FRIENDS FOREVER

WHEREVER WHENEVER

FRIENDS FOREVER
WHEREVER WHENEVER

A little book of
big appreciation

KAREN SALMANSOHN
BEST-SELLING AUTHOR OF *INSTANT HAPPY*

ILLUSTRATIONS BY KIM SIELBECK

TEN SPEED PRESS
California | New York

INTRODUCTION

There are millions of reasons to appreciate your friends. This fun book celebrates fifty of them—with feisty humor and lots of love.

If you've received this book as a gift, then congratulations! It's proof that you are deeply loved and appreciated. You have someone in your corner who is always there to cheer you on and cheer you up!

Lucky you!

After all, a good friendship is truly priceless—and that's backed by research. In one study, happiness researchers Ed Diener and Martin Seligman compared a group of very happy people to one of very unhappy people—and found that the first group was highly social and had the strongest relationship ties.

So if you feel like you're happier because a certain friend is in your life, well, that's a genuine feeling—backed up by science.

And if you're the one who bought this book, feel free to keep the friendship-appreciation love flowing and pass it on! Share it with a friend you know to show them how very happy they make you feel—and you'll then make them feel a little happier in the process.

So whether you have a big group of friends or a select scattering of besties, or you're still searching for your tribe, this book will celebrate the power of the special human connection that is friendship.

And I hope that when you're done reading this book, you'll consider me a friend too. With this in mind, feel free to reach out to me via the contact page on NotSalmon.com, and tell me a story about a special friend in your life. I might just share your story on my site to inspire others to be a good friend forever—wherever—whenever.

XO
Karen

I LOVE YOU MORE THAN
free Wi-Fi.

MY HOPE FOR YOU:

that life's winds of adversity
never blow off your
positive thinking cap.

MANY FRIENDS WILL BE THERE
WHEN TIMES ARE GOOD.

BUT IT'S DURING STORMY TIMES
THAT YOU FIND OUT WHO
HAS YOUR BACK . . .

and your umbrella.

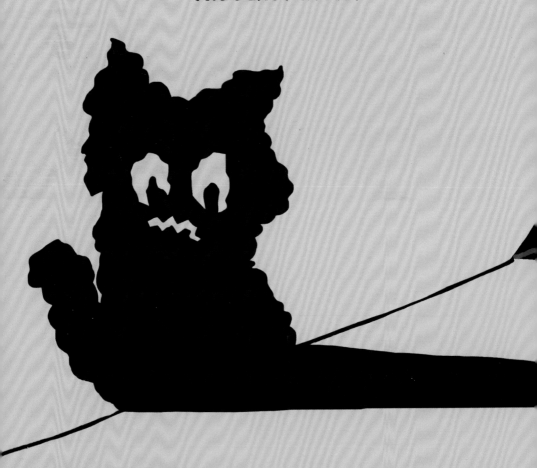

SOME PEOPLE BRING OUT
THE BEAST IN ME.

A FRIEND IS SOMEONE WHO
OVERLOOKS YOUR BROKEN FENCE
AND ADMIRES THE FLOWERS
IN YOUR GARDEN.

—proverb

YOUR **HUGS** CURE MY **UGHS.**

A TRUE FRIEND DOESN'T JUST SAY,

"Don't worry.
It will all be okay."

A TRUE FRIEND WILL TELL YOU:

"Yep. Things suck.
And things might suck
for a bit more."

THEN THEY'LL BRING YOU A
PINT OF ICE CREAM AND TWO SPOONS—
AND REMIND YOU THAT YOU
DON'T HAVE TO GO THROUGH THE
SUCK-ITUDE IN SOLITUDE.

YOU
DESERVE THE
BEST

YOU ROCK SO MUCH THAT YOU
boulder.

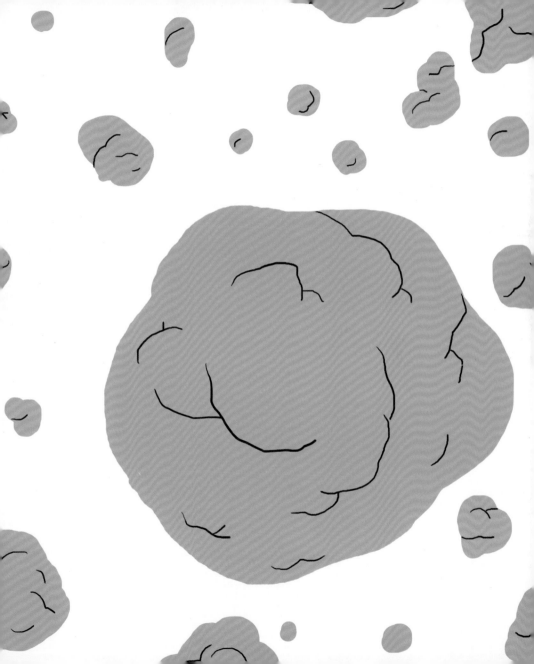

**I CAN NEVER STAY TOO MAD
AT YOU FOR TOO LONG,**

because we have too many
things to talk about!

I APPRECIATE HOW YOU
ALWAYS STRAIGHTEN MY CROWN
when it gets a little wobbly.

NO MATTER HOW SERIOUS LIFE GETS,

I know I can always
get silly with you!

I LOVE YOU MORE THAN COFFEE—

but not always before coffee.

YOU'RE WONDERFUL

AND

ANYBODY

WHO

DOESN'T LIKE YOU IS A BIG LAMEWAD.

ENOUGH SAID.

YOU DON'T NEED A CERTAIN NUMBER OF FRIENDS . . .

just a number of friends
you can be certain about.

A TRUE FRIEND SAYS GOOD THINGS
BEHIND YOUR BACK...

WHEN IT HURTS TO LOOK BACKWARD, AND I'M AFRAID TO LOOK FORWARD,

I just look at you beside me, and I feel much better.

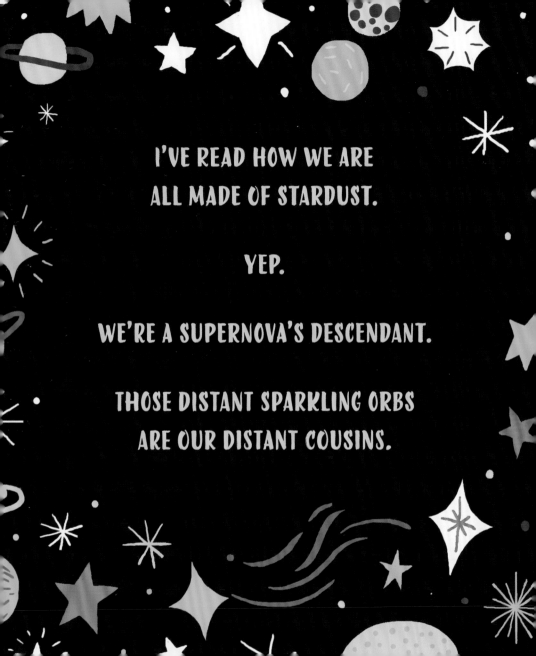

I'VE READ HOW WE ARE
ALL MADE OF STARDUST.

YEP.

WE'RE A SUPERNOVA'S DESCENDANT.

THOSE DISTANT SPARKLING ORBS
ARE OUR DISTANT COUSINS.

CRAZY TO THINK ABOUT—
EXCEPT IN YOUR CASE,
BECAUSE YOU ARE A

shining superstar!

YOU KNOW OUR FRIENDSHIP IS STRONG
BECAUSE WE CAN HAVE ENTIRE
CONVERSATIONS WITH EACH OTHER

simply by tagging
each other on memes.

SOMEONE ASKED ME
THE OTHER DAY IF
I BELIEVE MIND READERS
ARE A REAL THING.

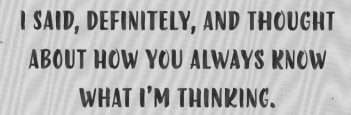

I SAID, DEFINITELY, AND THOUGHT
ABOUT HOW YOU ALWAYS KNOW
WHAT I'M THINKING.

(But of course you knew that!)

YOU MAKE ME FEEL
STRONGER THAN I AM

(and funnier than I am—
because you laugh at my
stupid jokes!).

I LOVE THAT YOU ARE HAPPY
FOR ME WHEN I AM HAPPY,
SAD FOR ME WHEN I AM SAD—

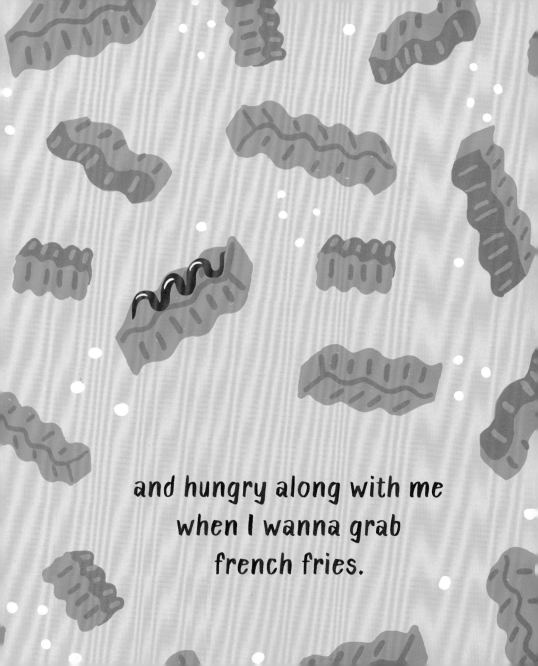

and hungry along with me
when I wanna grab
french fries.

FRIENDS COME AND GO
LIKE WAVES IN THE OCEAN,

but true friends stick like sand
to your bikini bottom.

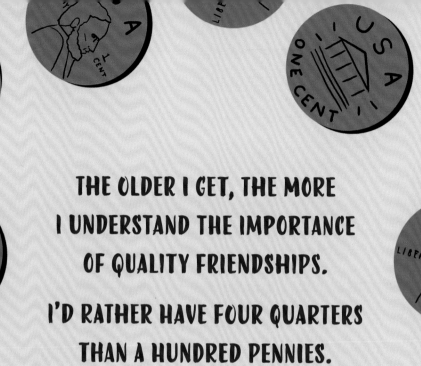

THE OLDER I GET, THE MORE
I UNDERSTAND THE IMPORTANCE
OF QUALITY FRIENDSHIPS.

I'D RATHER HAVE FOUR QUARTERS
THAN A HUNDRED PENNIES.

And you're one beautiful
shiny quarter.

YOU ARE MY HUMAN DIARY.
TOGETHER WE SHARE
HUNDREDS OF CRAZY STORIES,
THOUSANDS OF INSIDER SECRETS,
AND MILLIONS OF SILLY JOKES

(7,497,321 of which are
funny only to us).

MANY FRIENDS ARE LIKE
THE CLOUDS IN THE SKY—
THEY DRIFT IN AND OUT, AND OCCASIONALLY
RAIN ALL OVER YOUR PARADE.

But you're like the sky
behind the clouds—
true blue and infinitely
there for me.

WHEN YOU CAN'T LOOK
ON THE BRIGHT SIDE,

I will sit with you
in the dark.

YOU NOT ONLY KNOW MY STORIES,
YOU HELPED ME TO WRITE THEM

(and rewrite them—
and re-re-rewrite them)

TILL THEY ARE A LOT FUNNIER!

I WISH I COULD COPY AND PASTE YOU
wherever I go.

I APPRECIATE HOW YOU DO THINGS THAT COUNT ON COUNTLESS OCCASIONS

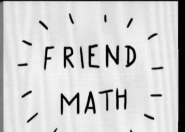

ONE LOYAL FRIEND IS WORTH
TEN THOUSAND RELATIVES.

—Euripides

THEY SAY YOU PICK UP THE GOOD HABITS
OF THE FIVE PEOPLE YOU SPEND
THE MOST TIME WITH.

I'd love to clone you four times!

A GOOD FRIEND DOUBLES THE GOOD TIMES

I LOVE HOW WE EACH ROOT FOR BLESSINGS TO HAPPEN FOR THE OTHER

and how we do what
we can to be each
other's blessings.

THANK YOU FOR PICKING
ME UP WHEN I FALL.

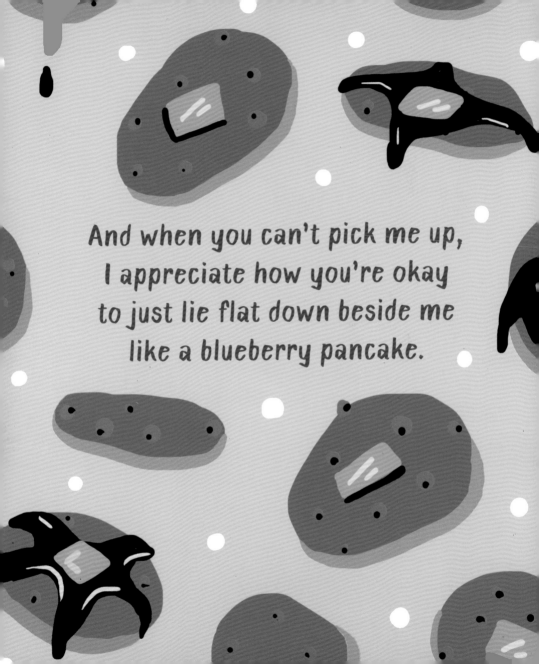

And when you can't pick me up,
I appreciate how you're okay
to just lie flat down beside me
like a blueberry pancake.

YOU'RE LIKE A UNICORN
WHO BRINGS ME
CHOCOLATE AND A LATTE—

too good to be true.

YOU: Where are you?

ONE OF THE BEST THERAPIES IS
TIME SPENT WITH A GOOD FRIEND.
AND IT'S CHEAPER TOO.

(Unless you go shopping.)

OUR FRIENDSHIP

OR MY JEANS FROM
COLLEGE

WE ALL REJOICE IN HEARING
THOSE THREE LITTLE WORDS:

I L<u>OV</u>E YOU

BENEATH THESE THREE LITTLE WORDS
ARE ANOTHER THREE LITTLE WORDS:

I G<u>E</u>T YOU

It's when you feel most understood
that you feel most loved.

YOU

ARE MADE OF
→ 100% ←
AWESOMESAUCE
♥
NO ARTIFICIAL INGREDIENTS

FRIENDSHIP FACTS

BASED ON 1 AMAZING
HUMAN   %

KINDNESS   100%

LOYALTY   100%

HONESTY   100%

GENEROSITY   100%

I DON'T THINK I SHOULD
CALL YOU A FRIEND—
AND THAT'S A COMPLIMENT.

I MEAN, LOOK AT THAT WORD
"friend."

IT HAS "END" INSIDE OF IT!
YOU'RE MORE LIKE A
"friforever."

I APPRECIATE HOW YOU
UNDERSTAND MY PAST,
BELIEVE IN MY FUTURE, AND
ACCEPT ME AS I AM TODAY . . .
EVEN ON BAD HAIR DAYS.

(And you admit to me that
I am having a bad hair day!)

I LOVE HOW I CAN
think out loud
IN FRONT OF YOU.

I APPRECIATE HOW YOU'RE THERE
WHEN I TELL YOU I NEED YOU—

AND EVEN WHEN I TELL YOU
THAT I DON'T NEED YOU . . .

but I really kinda do.

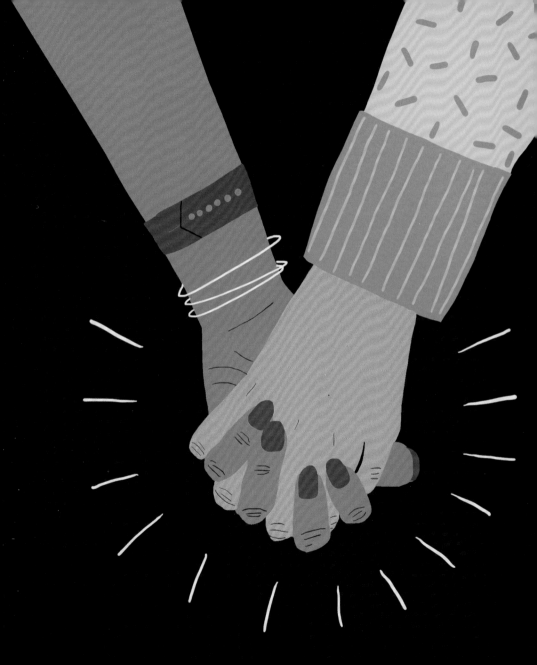

and so YES YES YES to YOU!

KIND

PEOPLE

ARE MY

KINDA

- PEOPLE -

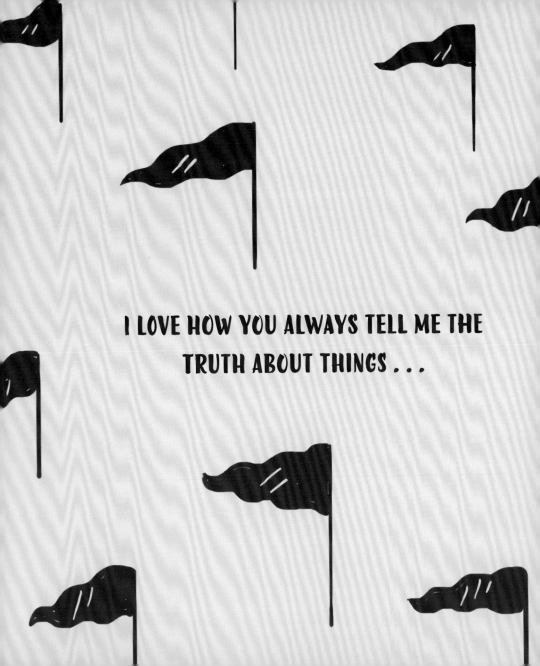

I LOVE HOW YOU ALWAYS TELL ME THE
TRUTH ABOUT THINGS . . .

even things I'm not truthful
to myself about.

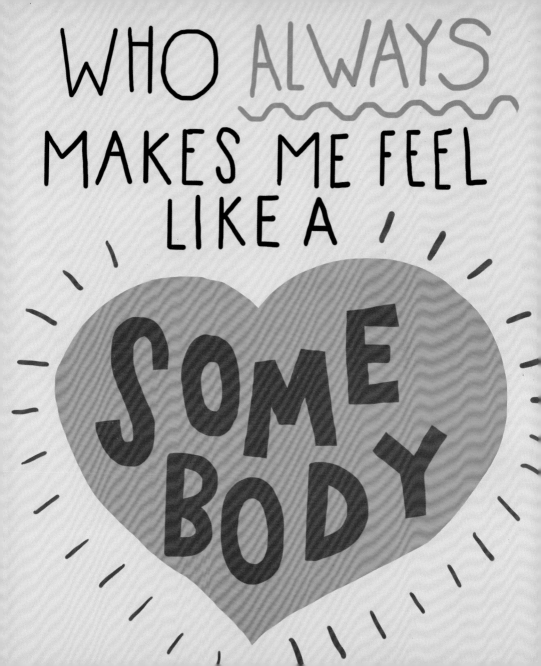

MY WISH FOR YOU:

May you know that
life's best opportunities often
arrive incognito as endings.

ACKNOWLEDGMENTS

Studies show that people are happier in their jobs—and lives—when they have good friendships with the people they work with.

In particular, Gallup reports that enjoying close work friendships boosts job satisfaction by 50 percent.

With this in mind, I'd love to acknowledge my appreciation for the folks whose friendships I got to experience while working on this friendship book—who helped to boost my job satisfaction not by 50 percent but more like 1,000,000 percent!

Sending a huge virtual hug and humongous thank you to this book's amazing team: my soulmate editor, Lisa Westmoreland; my sweet and talented designer, Chloe Rawlins; my brilliant and colorful illustrator, Kim Sielbeck; and my awesome agent entourage including Celeste Fine, Jaidree Braddix, Sarah Passick, and Anna Petkovich.

Plus I'd love to thank all the loving friends who keep my soul happily caffeinated: Ari Salmansohn, Howard Schwartz, Shelly Lipton, Danielle Pashko, Cory van den Bossche, Kristine Carlson, Bonnie Winston, Kristy Lin, Michael John Hughes, Karen Giberson, Richard Kastleman, Susan Shapiro, Safije Alija, Dominique Misrahi, Shely Katri, Denise Barry, Josselyne Herman Saccio, Berrnadette Penotti, Brigitte Nicole, Andrea Syrtash, Li Saul, Jennifer Pastiloff, Evan Cooper, Michaela Alexis, Lisa Attea, Marcia Bronstein, Gloria Salmansohn, Eric Salmansohn, Lia Salmansohn, Ross Salmansohn, and many others—too many to list, but you know who you are!

ABOUT THE AUTHOR

KAREN SALMANSOHN is a happiness and wellness expert who is the author of numerous best-selling self-empowerment books including *Instant Happy, Think Happy,* and *How to Be Happy, Dammit,* with more than one million copies sold. She has studied to be a yoga and meditation teacher at Ishta Yoga; founded the "DO IT Healthy Eating Programs," and created a range of life-boosting digital courses on MastersInLife.com. She's been featured on the *Today* show, *The View,* CNN, CNBC and *Real Time with Bill Maher;* served as a columnist for Oprah.com, *Psychology Today,* CNN, MSN, Yahoo!, AOL, Match, and *Huffington Post;* and been covered by the *New York Times, Business Week, Chicago Tribune, Los Angeles Times, Philadelphia Inquirer, Time, Marie Claire, Fast Company, InStyle, Self, ELLE,* and the *New Yorker.* She lives in New York, New York. Feel free to say a friendly howdy to her at NotSalmon.com and MastersInLife.com.

All rights reserved.
Published in the United States by Ten Speed Press,
an imprint of the Crown Publishing Group, a division
of Penguin Random House LLC, New York.
www.crownpublishing.com
www.tenspeed.com

Ten Speed Press and the Ten Speed Press
colophon are registered trademarks of
Penguin Random House LLC.

Library of Congress Cataloging-in-
Publication Data is on file with
the publisher.

Hardcover ISBN: 978-0-399-58100-7
eBook ISBN: 978-0-399-58101-4

Printed in China

Design by Chloe Rawlins
Author photograph by
Laura DeSantis-Olsson

10 9 8 7 6 5 4 3 2 1

First Edition

BEST FRIEND